George Washington

By Wil Mara

Consultants
Nanci R. Vargus, Ed.D.
Primary Multiage Teacher
Decatur Township Schools, Indianapolis, Indiana

Katharine A. Kane, Reading Specialist
Former Language Arts Coordinator
San Diego County Office of Education

Children's Press®
A Division of Scholastic Inc.
New York   Toronto   London   Auckland   Sydney
Mexico City   New Delhi   Hong Kong
Danbury, Connecticut

Designer: Herman Adler Design
Photo Researcher: Caroline Anderson
The photo on the cover shows George Washington.

Library of Congress Cataloging-in-Publication Data

Mara, Wil.
  George Washington / by Wil Mara.
    p. cm. — (Rookie biographies)
Includes index.
Summary: An introduction to the life of George Washington, who became the
first president of the United States after leading the American military in the
Revolutionary War against England.
  ISBN 0-516-22519-7 (lib. bdg.)   0-516-27335-3 (pbk.)
  1. Washington, George, 1732-1799—Juvenile literature. 2. Presidents—United
States—Biography—Juvenile literature. [1. Washington, George, 1732-1799.
2. Presidents.] I. Title. II. Series
  E312.66 .M27 2002
  973.4'1'092—dc21

                                    2001008318

George Washington was our first president.

4

He was born in Virginia on February 22, 1732.

Back then, America was ruled by England. Virginia was a colony, not a state. The people who lived in America were called colonists.

Washington's family owned a big farm. Young George enjoyed farm work.

He also liked to study. His favorite subject was math.

George Washington joined the military, or armed forces, when he was twenty years old. His first job was to deliver a note to a man more than three hundred miles away!

Washington left the military in 1759. Then he married Martha Custis.

He became a politician (pol-uh-TISH-uhn). A politician is elected, or chosen, to work for the government.

At this time, the English government began to tax the tea and stamps it sold to the American colonies. This made the colonists angry. They wanted to be free from England's laws.

A war began between England and the American colonies. It was called the Revolutionary (rev-uh-LOO-shuhn-air-ee) War. Washington was asked to lead the military during this war.

15

Washington was a good leader. The colonies won the war in 1783. America became a free country.

George Washington was a hero.

In 1789, he was elected to be
America's first president.

It was hard to be president of a new country. The government was very small.

Washington found smart and honest people to work with him.

Copyright, 1876, by Currier & Ives, N.Y. ALEXANDER HAMILTON, Secy. of the Treasury

GENL HENRY KNOX, Secy. of War.

GEORGE WASHINGTON. THOMAS JEFFERSON, Secy. of State.

EDMUND RANDOLPH, Attorney General.

WASHINGTON AND HIS CABINET.

CONTINENTAL DOLLAR
1776

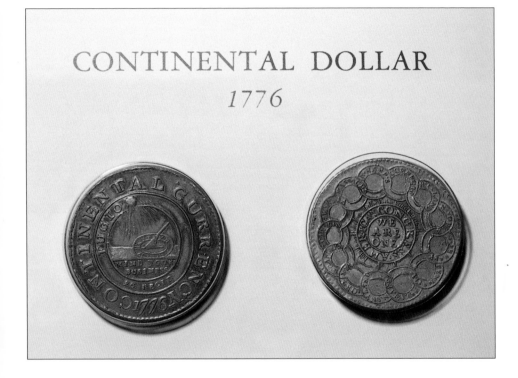

America also needed its
own money. There were no
American coins or paper bills.
Washington passed a law that
let the government make some.

Washington worked as president for four years. Then he wanted to go back to Virginia. But many people asked Washington to stay for four more years. He did.

25

Washington went back to Virginia to be with his family in 1797. He died there on December 14, 1799.

Today, we think of George Washington as "The Father of Our Country."

America's capital city, Washington, D.C., is named after him.

Words You Know

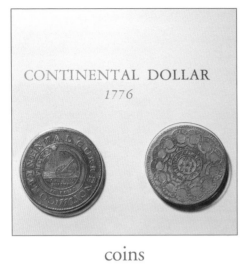

coins

colonists

hero

military

president

George Washington

Washington, D.C.

31

Index

About the Author

Wil Mara has written over fifty books. He writes fiction and nonfiction for both children and adults. He lives with his wife and three daughters in northern New Jersey.

Photo Credits

Photographs © 2002: Art Resource, NY: cover; Bridgeman Art Library International Ltd., London/New York: 25, 31 left (Brooklyn Museum of Art, New York, USA), 11 (Private Collection); Hulton Archive/Getty Images: 18, 30 bottom left; North Wind Picture Archives: 8, 15, 26, 30 bottom right; Photo Researchers, NY/Library of Congress: 21; Photri Inc.: 16, 22, 29, 30 top left, 31 bottom left; Stock Montage, Inc.: 7, 12, 30 top right; Superstock, Inc.: 3 (New Bedford Public Library), 4 (Philadelphia Free Library/A.K.G. Berlin), 19, 31 top left.

This Rookie Biography teaches young readers about George Washington, the first president of the United States. Learn about Washington's first job in the military and how he helped form the United States government after leading the colonists to victory in the Revolutionary War.

Read these other Rookie Biographies™

Abraham Lincoln

Alexander Graham Bell

Amelia Earhart

Benjamin Franklin

Clara Barton

Harriet Tubman

Jackie Robinson

John Muir

Martin Luther King Jr.

2.6

U.S. $4.95
Can. $7.95

ISBN 0-516-27335-3

90000

9 780516 273358

CHILDREN'S PRESS

SCHOLASTIC